# Flying Strongly On One Wing

## a poem about the other wing

# by

# orde

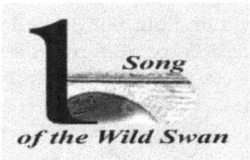

Song

*of the Wild Swan*

Published by Song, 2014.
Song is an Imprint of:
Song of the Wild Swan Ltd.
1 Folly Bridge, Oxford, OX1 4LB, UK.
www.songwildswan.com
tel +44 (0) 1865 240572
fax +44 (0) 1865 246565
e: info@songwildswan.com

**Flying Strongly on One Wing** by orde
ISBN 9781909777132

First published: 1985 (Private, 30 copies).
eBook: 2014 Song, Oxford.

# Acknowledgements

Song eBook Design series by Laurence Hutton-Smith.
Cover Design: Laurence Hutton-Smith.
Cover Image: *Eagle Owl*, photograph by Laurence Hutton-Smith, © 2014
Laurence Hutton-Smith.
Book Production: Amaury Marinho Junior

# Contents

# FLYING STRONGLY ON ONE WING

a poem about the other wing.

"Time was away and somewhere else"

## . I .

What is the other wing
I asked.
I waited.
softness .
I was open
waiting.
ya.
it was no word, but a sound.
soft too.
the eyes
always those goddamn eyes.
if only I could see through them
a friend once said to me.
it was so soft a sound.
a sound so soft after waiting.
she took her time so that

all the time the softness could
grow.
I hardly recall the word, for
I recall only the feeling.
a smile she had too, a
soft smile.
what is the other wing?

" now is the time for the burning of
                        the leaves "

## II.

softly softly you knew what
the other wing is.
softly softly does it seem.

" I sing what was lost and dread
                    what was won "

## III.

NO.
for I see no other wing.
I am soft I am open

I am ready willing and able
to fly.
another wing. yes. maybe.
it is growing or, to be grown.
but the other wing
what is the other wing
stronger now.
what is the other wing
I want to know.

" can they still live "

## IV.

a look soft she comes
she come to me.
The tentative one.
down down. don't like say I.
down down you stirrings
in my heart.
don't like.
don't like.
the tentative one. How my heart

fills. she is the one. the
one.

I ask myself. why do I
cover   why do I cover
immediately my dislike . why
do I cover so quick my
heart. who do I say: don't
like. so quickly. involuntarily.
the tentative one.

" Be not so desolate "

## V

she is   help
she is   acknowledgement
she is   care
she is   appreciation
she is   the simple things
she is   love
she is   enjoyment
she is   fun
she is   lightheartedness

she is a bird who enjoys
enjoy
enjoy.
tentative one. who are you.
she is fragile
she is kind
she is small
she is twice
she is a dove
held in my hand with such
tenderness
such tenderness in ~~my~~ mine eyes.
she is a dove
a dove lying in my hand
in the palm. tender, warm.
her heart beating warmly. I
can feel it. what do I do
with this dove.
she is so vulnerable.

" When a man has cast out fear"
VI

she is a word to the wise.
a word one can use.
legable.
what is it, one does not
think so well, what is it
that is of rich — rish
looking.
legable.
one is try to cope.
no. the wing is strong.
it beats.
coping.

"I am the land of their fathers."

## VII

silence. or is it my imagination
the words stream at me
a short steady flow.
you do cope.
Boy, do you pay a price.
price?

price?
is there a price to be set on
the strong.
but it is I who am saying
my own price.
I'm prepared to pay the price.

" Call to the swan and bid him bring"

<u>VIII</u>.

you.
and only.
and have not — for you only
have one heart.
oh heart.
you are breaking.
I feel my heart is breaking
care.
and care.
need to take care.
you only have one set parents.

open ?
open heart to them.
they need to protect themselves.
open enough ?
open enough to see your
heart, you lose your
protection.
you drop that and
and at a very real
level you can cope.
yes
yes I can
but
there's a point at
which a point at
which you don't cope.
paper over
paper cracks
paper over the cracks.
cracks.

"we are the hollow men"

## IX

the coping part.
can't take away.
very serious coping
part
can't subvert that.
you drop that and
they
they can't respond
appropriately.
open enough to see your
heart.
you lose protection.
open enough to see your
heart, you lose your
protection.
they can't respond appropriately
very disilitioning.
another heartbreak.
another heartbreak.

## X

Poems of our time
1900 —
everyman.
I will go with thee
and be thy guide,
In thy most need
to go by thy side

"these, in the day when heaven
was falling"

## XI

Ah yes — protection.
a band of protection hurts.
you drop it to see your
heart.
you are open enough
you need to take care
Oh yes
you drop that and they
can't respond appropriately.

protecting them and try
try get something
from them.
Trust

Trust

TRUST —they protect
themselves.

the problem, the problem
yes the problem is so
simple.

they protect themselves so well
that they hurt.

I fight

I fight straight
straight enough to not
tolerate excuses.

I can't pretend it does
not matter to me.

It matters enough.

It matters

it matters enough
because I; I

schlep across.
not pretend it does not
matter —
help.
help them.
help them to give me what
I need.
it will not harm them.

" speech after long silence; it
is right "

## XII

these were words
but none so —
they were action words
wrought from the heart
words and actions
feelings and thoughts
on the table
open and trying
so hard

so hard.
rely on me more
I need you to rely on me
more.
you know why? I question
her.
why?
a large reply
because she could.
   "    she could.
   "    they could.
   "    I can.
   "    I love.
said so much.
said so much in these
words.
words of attempted
understanding.
trying trying to bridge
words to actions
words to understand
feelings beyond.

because I was there.
there.
because I thought about her.
because I got her a ....
because I spent a lot of...
because I got grapes.
grapes
and so on
along the line.
she.
she turned to me.
she had not turned
away.
she was there in
front of me.
trying to feed
blood into the
other being:—
they gave you something
they gave you what
they could.
thank them for trying.

" His eyes are quickened
so with grief "

<u>XIII</u>

NO.
no I don't think they
they tried to
understand what I
needed.
I think they pretended.
But :—
even that is sufficient.
even that is sufficient.
it's that bad.
the pretence was sufficient.


" you, you are all unloving,
lovelers, you "

<u>XIV</u>

you you you dare

not pretend.
only here you dare
not pretend.
not do.
if
it means.
weep, wail.
if it really means pretence.
breaking down.
thats the block.
    "    the barrier.
    "    it.


" Nor dread nor hope attend "


<u>XV</u>


well,
we'll see
how long it
lasts.

"Glory is of the sun, too, and the sun of suns."

## XVI.

I agree said I.
I agree with you.
can I afford to I asked.
yes I agree I can.
its not.
its not a question said I.
its not a question will I.
its a question of will it
the _pretence_ of.
of what.
that.
that I
that I have been hunt.
so what.
that's not the issue.
   "        "     "        " .
I know that.

I acknowledge it.
anyway,
I'm all in favour of
dropping pretensions.
anyway,
you are not giving
me a hard
time.
you are not,
I want to fly
to fly on
both wings.
I'm searching anyway
I'm searching
desperately
for the other wing.

" Tempt me no more; for I "

<u>XVII</u>

so she said
so my love

she said
to accept.
O.K. so accept.
I've been hurt.
I don't know
if I've been hurt.
I feel hurt.
hold fast.
I dare not pretend what.
oh ugh — she breaks
through.
oh my god how I do
ugh — tears come
like wells from
the ground —
struck by the rod.
answer me that she
whispers — outside
she is concerned
she feels I need
fresh air
to fly.

no its not that bad
I can cope
I can fly
strongly even
I can can fly strongly
and even.
flying.

" Lord, the roman hyacinths
are blooming in bowls
and "

## XVIII

3 words
every thing
3 words came
I asked someone
come into head.
ask
3 words came.

she looked
and said :-
its not that simple.
she looked.
at a very real level
you can cope.
she flowed.
yes I can.
but she flowed.
there's a point at
which you don't cope.
there's a point at
which — paper over
the cracks.


" In the strange isle "

<u>XIX</u>


can't
can't take away

the very serious coping
part.
can't subvert that.

" He stood, and heard the
steeple' "

$$\overline{XX}$$

sorry, can't agree.
with that
I'm not interested
in whether I need
that coping part
or whether it
shouldn't be subverted
because I feel
it should be
should be
subverted.
no question.

i don't believe that
its valuable to have
that.
i'd rather fall
than pretend to stand.
thats all.
its really very
simple.


"sitting in this garden you
cannot escape symbols"

<u>XXI</u>

descent.

Either
either
either i sink or swim.
you believe i'll swim.
i have no option.

" Speech after long silence; it
is right, "

**XXII**

Either I do or don't,
But I don't want to,
go on as is.
Its not right.
It isn't.
I don't care if its important
or not.
Its not right.
whats not right.
Its not right.
whats not right.

" and then I pressed the shell "

**XXIII**

pretense.
I said. I'd rather
fall
than pretend to
stand.
uh uh.

am I vulnerable?
I feel O.K.
can I cope?
I still think so.
and what price?
who do I cope?
do I need to pretend?
to cope, and if so why?
I don't pretend I cope.
of course I feel the
pain.
is there anything I
can do about it?
the pain that is.
NO

But that's not pretence,
there's nothing I
can do about it.
except feel it.
anything do to
avoid it —
answer has to
be no
must be yes to
the answer.
can one avoid it.
No.
I don't think ever
denied feel pain.

" there going home at dusk "

## XXIV

surrender to it.
ie. saying ouch.
say ouch.

how?
of course says
ouch inside.
of course one feels that.
perhaps question
is to say —
stuff that.
to hell with them.
i'm not going to
put up with that.
may have to
put up with it.
most do. best
can do is to
cry out.
cry out what.
ouch.

" nobody, ancient mischief, nobody"

XXV

Jews

are lucky
can say oi vay.
no
that's mind not feeling.
such its painful
having, having a
broken wing.
can't
beyond pain.
unless
cry out.
is something
beyond pain?
beyond pain
new jerusalem.
acceptance.
a sort of humbling
a kind of joining
the rest of human
race.
can't be their lot.
it is.

pain?
not pain
must be more
 "         "        "
It isn't all pain
I won't accept 50/50
"       "
"       "    .
when there's pain
nothing else counts.
thats where I am
at the moment.
the pain of flying
on one wing.
even strongly.
and so.
try apple tart
if you can.
I can
ya.
even if I have to.

" 'When I'm alone' — the words
tripped off his tongue."

## XXVI

whats political
withdraw.
desperation about
feelings — when
things go — must
go whole way.
no compromise.
why should
one compromise ones
feelings.
no contact.
doesn't sound right

neither does compromise.
compromise or withdraw,
withdraw
with occasional
sorties.

Does that sound
familiar.
yes.
is that wrong?
lovely coffee.
what's the alternative.
crying on outside as
well as on inside.
I recommend it
with all my heart.

" I am the land of their fathers."

## XXVII

I'd like to say I'll try.
I'll try.
I wonder how low
I am.
Ability
drag back
from precipice.
come edge

feel terror.
what is that
edge.
over edge
loss control
loss familiarity.

" man is a sacred city
built of marvellous earth.

## XXVIII

familiarity time
our lives.
atmosphere represents
fall
from grace
always, fall into it —
safe on top
nothing scary.
fall
interesting history
fall, paradise.

loss of innocence
loss of illusion
et après
le déluge.
I'm not afraid of it.
no
I want it
you " it.
loss of pride
goes with fall.
I saw my mother
fall.
How
was that for you.
human.
pleasing.
triumph is too strong.
awareness.
I don't care who
triumphs if I
fall.
all I care is

understanding.
sounds great.

" say this when you return "

$$\overline{XIX}$$

fall into what.
what
          "

          "

usually into shit.
whats shit.
its nervy.
no thats illusion.
so what.
that's the appearance.
what's the reality?
being ill
is falling into —
maybe
being ill is what.

loss of face
"      "      "
well
so what
      "    's the centre
      "    "      "      "
humanity.
uh uh

anyway so what.
" what is the other wing "

---
xxx
---

where am ?
flying.
home or out?
home is the heart, anyway
the other wing
the wing that feels
one can fly without
feeling.

to find that wing
"      "      "      "
it isn't even that,
one can or can't
is it
is it right.

# Note by the Publisher 2013

| Mæg ic be me sylfum | I can make a true song |
|---|---|
| soðgied wrecan, | about me myself, |

The Seafarer, date unknown.(Approximate translation of the old English)

Song, established in 2013  is an imprint of a new publication House, a division of Song of the Wild Swan Ltd.

It publishes any writings from anyone who has a song.

Song also participates in the BEL (Barter Exchange Levy) Price System.

## List of Selected Works by orde

Song, November 2013
*Areas of classification may overlap*

### Books

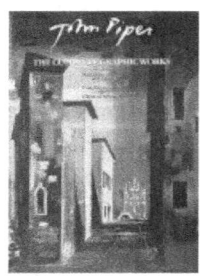

1   *John Piper – The Complete Graphic Works: A Catalogue Raisonné 1923-1983.* Compiled and edited by Orde Levinson. Faber & Faber, 1988.

2   *I Was Lonelyness: The Complete Graphic Works of John Muafangejo 1968-1987.* Struik Winchester, 1992. Foreword by Archbishop Desmond Tutu. Contributing essays from: Olga Levinson (The Life and Art of John Muafangejo); Edward Lucie-Smith (John Muafangejo); Pat Gilmour (On Not Being a Political Artist); Orde Levinson (John Muafangejo, Cubism and Traditional African

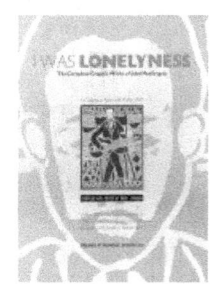

Art); Olga Levinson (The Historical Development of Art in Namibia) and Steven Sack (The Rorke's Drift Art and Craft Centre) and all Muafangejo's Interviews, Statements and published conversations.

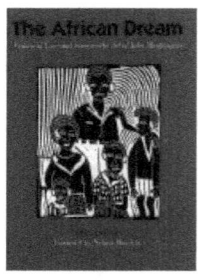

3   *The African Dream – Visions of Love and Sorrow. The Art Of John Muafangejo.* Thames and Hudson, 1993. Foreword by Nelson Mandela.

4   *Quality and Experiment. The Prints of John Piper – A Catalogue Raisonné.* Lund Humphries, 1996.

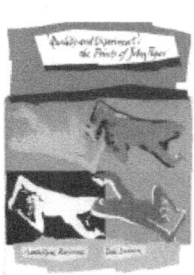

5   *The Prints of John Piper – A Catalogue Raisonné 1921-1991.* Lund Humphries, 2010. Contributing essays: Introduction (Orde Levinson); Experiment and Quality (Orde Levinson); Subject and Technique in Piper's Printmaking (David Fraser Jenkins); Working with Printers (John Piper).

6    *Hitting the Nail on the Head – The Complete Written Works of John Piper 1913-1992.* An estimated three volumes with contributing essays by various authors (tba). Scheduled for publication 2014/5.

7    *Delights and Aphorisms, selected writings of John Piper.* Scheduled for publication 2014-5.

8    *Daniel Henry Kahnweiler: A bibliography.* Scheduled for publication 2014.

9    *The Life and Work of Daniel Henry Kahnweiler: A critical evaluation.* Originally part of the D. Phil. Study at Magdalen College, Oxford University. Scheduled for publication 2015.

10   *The Complete Writings of Daniel Henry Kahnweiler.* Three volumes. Scheduled for publication 2015-6.

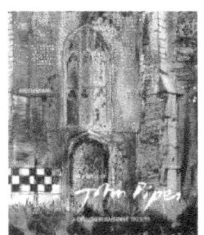
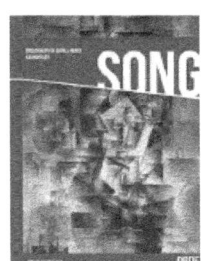

**Conversations and interviews**

11   *orde's Conversations with Henry Moore.* Henry Moore talks about influences, the artists he likes, his work and life in general. Available as eBook 2013  Book published by Song 2014

12   *Orde's Conversations with Richard Sorabji (videoed)* in progress,. Richard Sorabji in thought and in person is brought to us in a unique experiment where orde has selected friends from each decade to converse with him. Completed to date are Louis Hynes (age 10);

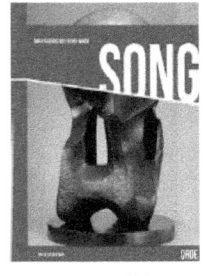

Laurence Hutton-Smith (age 20); Richard Kuziara (age 37); Lisa Hammond-Marty (age 40-50); Jeremy Rowe (age 50-58); Marianne Talbot (age 58--68)  Joanna Foster (age 68-80). Available as video, eBook and book. Scheduled publication 2015.

13   *Talking to Solly Irwin (videoed)*
     Schedule publication as eBook and book 2014-5,

## Films

14    *Essences.* Independent production produced by orde under the inspiration of Straub and Huillet. A contemplative mood piece starring Richard E. Grant and Kiki Savejan
Director/script/editor: orde
Cast: Richard E Grant, Kiki Savejan
Running Time: 40 minutes/colour
Date Completed: 1983
(Image: Scene Shot from Essences by orde.)

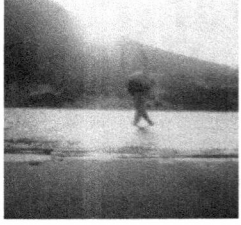

15    *Ÿ*
Director/script/editor: orde
Cast: Richard E Grant
Running time:16 minutes/colour
Date Completed: c.1987.

## Film scripts

16    *The Judgment of Shylock.* In progress.

## In fermentation/digestion

17    *The Inventors dilemma.* A novel?
18    *Five Fingers are not the same.* A novel?
19    *Turquoise.* A love story.
20    *The Weather of myself.* A philosophical book/diary.
21    *The Human Tragedy.* A true story, novel/poem?

## Music

22    *I am here thank you please, a musical composition.* Contains an introduction on classical and romantic by orde.
Available 2014 as eBook and book (published by Song.

23    *Le Bordel Philosophique.* A musical composition with 5 contemporary composers (George Barton, Sam Fernando, Cheryl Francis-Hoad, Simon Roth, Jaime Wolfson). A composition based on a poem, which is based on a painting to reach a musical gesamtkunstwerk for our era. Scheduled for completion 2014.

## Plays

24      *Forcible Love*. A play based on the life of John
        Muafangejo.

25      *Forcible Love (NTN version)*. A musical on the
        life of John Muafangejo - premiered at the
        National Theatre, Windhoek, Namibia for the
        Independence Celebrations. Includes reviews.
        Available 2014 as eBook and book (published
        by Song)

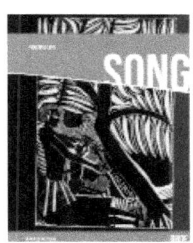

26      *The Rialto Dialogues*. Described as a
        revolutionary work about the Merchant of
        Venice by William Shakespeare. It includes the
        entire work uncut but introduces 4 new
        characters to open a meaning and channel to
        one of Shakespeare's greatest plays.
        Available 2014 as eBook and book (published
        by Song)

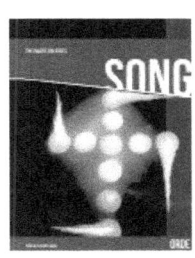

27      *Shylock the Magnificent*. A play 13 years after
        the Trial Scene of the Merchant of Venice by Shakespeare.
        Available 2014 as eBook and book (published by Song)
        See also The Soul's Heritage under poems.

## Poems

28      *Miscellaneous poems*. Short poems found over
        the years.
        Available 2014 as eBook and book.

29      *The Love song of D. Adolph Hitler*. In progress.

30      *Der Tod Des Miguel*. In progress

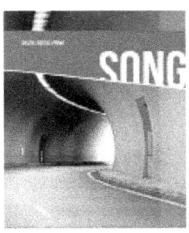

31      *Les Dem*. About Picasso's painting *Les Demoiselles D'Avignon*,
        includes essay on *Les Dem* by Professor Andrew Laird.
        Available 2014 as eBook and book (published by Song).

32      *Ndilapa Nkosi*. A lyrical comedy, first part of *The Soul's Heritage*, a
        trilogy, a landmark work described by Samuel Beckett as a
        'moving feat'. Includes reviews and responses from various persons
        including Beckett.

Available 2014 as eBook and book (published by Song).

33    *Antomat Diplony of the Orb.* An epic comedy, in progress, second part of The Soul's Heritage, a trilogy.

34    *The Argonauta Vineyard.* A tragic comedy, in progress, third part of The Soul's Heritage, a trilogy.

35    *Parlez à Voir.*
      Available 2014 as eBook and book (published by Song).

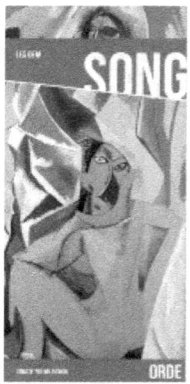

36    *Flying strongly on one wing.*
      Available 2014 as eBook and book (published by Song).

37    *Snowflakes and Ashes.*
      Available 2014 as eBook and book (published by Song).

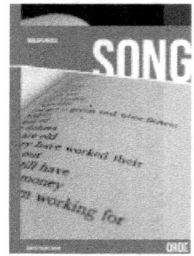

## Reviews and articles

38    A number of articles and reviews exist and are being collated.

39    *Art, An Adaptive Function?*
      Encyclopaedia of Evolution Mark Pagel (Editor-in-Chief), Oxford University Press, 2002. (365 articles from 330 different authors).

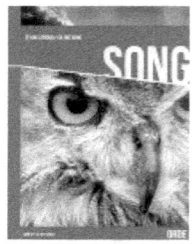

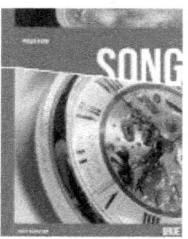

## Visual works

Drawings, paintings, photography, prints, sculptures
Please see www.orde.info